MISSION IN THE JUNGLE

A play by Dianne Irving
Illustrated by Adele K. Thomas

Contents

Pearson Australia
(a division of Pearson Australia Group Pty Ltd)
707 Collins Street, Melbourne, Victoria 3008
PO Box 23360, Melbourne, Victoria 8012
www.pearson.com.au

2019 2018 2017 2016
10 9 8 7 6 5 4 3 2 1

Text by Dianne Irving
Illustrations by Adele K. Thomas

Publishers: Sabine Bolick, Beth Zeme
Project Managers: Diane Leyman, Michelle Thomas
Lead Editor: Steve Dobney
Editor: Sally Green
Proofreader: Thalia Kalkipsakis
Designer: Lisa Howard
Senior File & Asset Coordinator: Rob Curulli
Cover art: Adele K. Thomas
Printed by SOS Print + Media Group

ISBN 978 1 4886 1314 2

Pearson Australia Group Pty Ltd
ABN 40 004 245 943

Characters

Ms Blunt

(secret agent)

Mr Sharp

(chief secret agent)

Akio

(Kira's twin)

Kira

(Akio's twin)

Sandra

Alex

Scene 1

Kira and Akio have arrived in Shavinder Jungle to meet Mr Sharp.

Mr Sharp: Good morning, secret agents.

Kira: Hi, Mr Sharp. This is so exciting. The holidays were getting pretty boring and we were looking for something to do.

Mr Sharp: Your parents nominated you for this job. I hope you're ready for a challenge.

Akio: We're more than ready. I like school holidays, but missions are the best.

Kira: We can't wait to get started! What **is** our mission, Mr Sharp?

Mr Sharp: Our task is to locate a box. It's important that it doesn't fall into the wrong hands.

Akio: Why is it so important?

Mr Sharp: It contains top-secret information about a rare species of plant.

Kira: Why is it top-secret?

Mr Sharp: This plant can be used to make a medicine that will save millions of lives. Unfortunately, some people want to control the medicine so they can charge a high price and make lots of money.

Akio: How will we find the box?

Mr Sharp: We have some clues. We found this map that marks a small clearing in the jungle.

Kira: Oh, it's like a treasure hunt. How exciting!

Mr Sharp: Here are your packs for the mission. They should have everything you need.

Akio: *(yawns)* Why did we need to start so early?

Mr Sharp: We have to be smart, just like the animals that live in the jungle. They're active at dawn and dusk because it's so hot during the day.

Akio: Will any other secret agents be helping us?

Mr Sharp: Not this time. We think that someone at the agency is trying to steal the box.

Kira: Does that mean you don't trust anyone else?

Mr Sharp: Exactly! I especially don't trust Ms Blunt, even though she has a security clearance.

Kira: I've always thought there was something not right about her.

Mr Sharp: I think Ms Blunt has turned bad, so we need to find the box before she does.

Kira: Is anyone with Ms Blunt?

Mr Sharp: Yes, Sandra and Alex.

Akio: We'd better be careful. We don't want to bump into them.

Scene 2

Meanwhile, Sandra, Alex and Ms Blunt are on a track in another part of the jungle.

Sandra: Stop complaining, Alex.

Alex: It feels like elephants have stomped on my feet.

Sandra: You're wearing the wrong shoes.

Alex: Yeah, but they look cool, don't they?

Ms Blunt: Stop whingeing! I've heard Kira and Akio are here with Mr Sharp on a mission to find a box. The agency believes that he's turned bad, so we need to make sure we get that box.

Sandra: How will we find it?

Ms Blunt: It's obvious, isn't it? We follow Mr Sharp and the twins.

Alex: Are you sure Mr Sharp is crooked?

Ms Blunt: Yes, as crooked as a dog's back leg.

Sandra: I've always thought there was something not right about him.

Scene 3

On a different track, Kira, Akio and Mr Sharp are whispering to one another.

Akio: Do you think that Alex and Sandra have turned bad too?

Mr Sharp: It's possible. Just remember: don't trust anyone!

Kira: We should try to stay out of their sight.

Mr Sharp: Yes, but we need to keep moving, so we'll use camouflage. That's how animals like the three-toed sloth survive in the jungle. They use camouflage to hide from predators. They need it, too, because they're one of the slowest animals in the world!

Kira: (*giggles*) Like you when you're getting ready for school, Akio!

Akio: (*frowning*) Ha ha.

Mr Sharp: There's a camouflage jacket and hat in your pack. Put them on. They'll help us blend in with the jungle.

Scene 4

Alex, Sandra and Ms Blunt continue on their track.

Alex: Oh, yuck, this is disgusting!

Ms Blunt: What's wrong now, Alex?

Alex: The humidity is unbearable. I'm sweating so much that it's messing up my hair.

Sandra: I have a hairbrush you can use.

Ms Blunt: I don't know how you two ever became secret agents.

Sandra: Well, I do know a lot of things. For example, I know how jungle plants catch water to survive. Some plants have a trumpet shape. They trap water in the bottom and this becomes a home for frogs and lizards.

Alex: Oh, gross! I don't even want to think about frogs and lizards.

Sandra: That's not the gross part –

Ms Blunt: Shh! We must find the twins. Stop talking, and remember: don't trust anyone!

Scene 5

Kira, Akio and Mr Sharp stop and look at the map.

Akio: Which way, Kira?

Kira: *(points)* The map shows we should go this way, towards a cave.

Mr Sharp: Let's stop in the cave for a moment. It will be a lot cooler.

Alex, Sandra and Ms Blunt appear on the same track, behind the others.

Sandra: *(whispering)* Look, there are the twins. They're wearing camouflage.

Alex: I can hardly see them.

Ms Blunt: That's such an old trick. They could have just used mud as camouflage – that's what some animals do.

Alex: That's disgusting. I'm not covering myself in mud.

Sandra: Well, we'll have to be really careful they don't see us. We'll be like jungle cats stalking their prey.

Kira, Akio and Mr Sharp reach the entrance of the cave.

Kira: Do you think there are bats inside?

Mr Sharp: I'd say it's likely. They're nocturnal, so they only come out at night. During the day they find a cool, dark place to hide. Take out the torch from your pack.

Akio: What is the first thing a bat learns at school?

Kira: I don't know, Akio. What?

Akio: The alpha-bat!

Kira: *(groans)* Your jokes are so bad.

Akio: Where do you think the others are?

Mr Sharp: I don't know, but I have a feeling we're being followed.

Mr Sharp, Akio and Kira enter the cave. Alex, Sandra and Ms Blunt remain outside.

Sandra: They've gone into the cave.

Ms Blunt: We can wait out here. We'll easily see them come out.

Alex: I'm happy to stay outside. The cave is probably full of creepy crawlies.

Sandra: Don't you know there are lots of insects and spiders in the jungle? They're probably all around us right now.

Alex: Oh, don't say that! Creepy crawlies give me nightmares.

Sandra: Look! Here they come. It looks like they're heading up the hill towards the waterfall.

Scene 6

The twins and Mr Sharp reach the waterfall. The others follow without being seen.

Kira: Look how muddy the path is around the waterhole. The others will see our footprints.

Akio: The water doesn't look very deep. If we wade across to the other side, they won't be able to track us.

Kira: Great idea.

Mr Sharp: Did you two know that jaguars are good swimmers?

Akio: What should you do if you find a jaguar sleeping on your bed?

Kira: I don't know. What should I do?

Akio: Sleep on the couch!

Kira: *(laughs)* That joke's even lamer than the last one.

The twins and Mr Sharp wade into the waterhole. Sandra, Alex and Ms Blunt remain on the muddy path.

Ms Blunt: I hope we're nearly at the box. I can't listen to many more pathetic jokes.

Sandra: I think they're hilarious.

Alex: Are we wading across the waterhole, too?

Ms Blunt: No, the track is much quicker and we don't need to hide our footprints.

Alex: That's a relief. I don't want to get my clothes wet.

Sandra: Alex, just be careful you don't –

Alex: AAAAHH!

Sandra: – slip!

Alex slips over in the mud.

Alex: Oh no! My clothes are ruined. I'm covered in slimy mud.

Sandra: Now you're camouflaged too!

Alex: It's not funny, Sandra.

Sandra: *(laughs)* Brown is **definitely** not your colour.

Ms Blunt: Be quiet, you two. They'll hear us.

Mr Sharp, Akio and Kira have started walking on a track on the other side of the waterhole. They stop suddenly.

Akio: Did you hear that scream?

Kira: It sounded like Alex.

Akio: They must be nearby. We'd better speed up.

Mr Sharp: What does the map show?

Kira: I'm not sure. The waterhole has put us off course.

Akio: This is a disaster. The others could beat us to the clearing now.

Alex, Sandra and Ms Blunt are still on the muddy path.

Sandra: We've lost them!

Alex: Maybe we should've crossed the waterhole after all.

Ms Blunt: No, this is the right way and I think we're ahead of them.

Sandra: How do you know it's the right way?

Ms Blunt: I can see a clearing up ahead. I think that's where the others are heading.

Alex: What exactly are we looking for?

Ms Blunt: My sources indicate that we're looking for a small, locked box.

Alex: Your sources? Do you mean our orders aren't from the agency?

Ms Blunt: Er, yes ... I meant the officers at the agency. Focus, Alex.

Sandra: This is exciting. I think we're going to get there first.

Alex: I do love beating others to the prize!

Ms Blunt: Well, then get cracking and get to that box first!

Alex: Sandra, you'll have to run. I can't run with all this mud sticking to me!

Sandra: It's lucky I'm wearing the agency's latest version of super runners.

Sandra races towards the clearing.

Mr Sharp and the twins are close behind the others.

Akio: I can see Sandra running up ahead! She's going to beat us to the clearing!

Kira: Oh no! They're going to get there first.

Mr Sharp: Yes, they probably are, but don't worry. They don't have the map. See here, it shows a big tree in the clearing. Why do you think they would show that particular tree?

Kira: The box must be buried near that tree! But there aren't any trees in the clearing.

Mr Sharp: Not any more. But look at the edge of the clearing. There's a huge tree that's fallen down. I would guess the box is there.

Kira: Akio, you go alone. You're the school running champion. You'll be much faster without us.

Akio runs after Sandra, heading towards the clearing.

Sandra arrives at the clearing first.

Sandra: I won! ... Now what do I do?

Akio reaches the fallen tree and begins digging just as the others reach the clearing.

Akio: I found the box, Mr Sharp!

Ms Blunt: Oh no, you don't! The box is **mine**! I'm going to sell the information and then I'll be rich! *(She laughs, snatches the box from Akio and pulls out a goo gun.)* Stay away from me or I'll spray you all with my goo gun.

Sandra: So **she's** the one who's as crooked as a dog's back leg.

Alex: Quick, Sandra! Use the hairbrush!

Mr Sharp: Hairbrush?

Sandra: Ah, yes! Unfortunately for you, Ms Blunt, I have my own secret weapon. This will stop you.

Sandra points her hairbrush at Ms Blunt.

Mr Sharp: Oh, that's brilliant, Sandra. Your hairbrush shoots out a net. You've trapped this rogue agent like a bug in a spider's web.

Alex: Ew, please, I don't like bugs.

Ms Blunt: Let me go!

Sandra: Definitely not! We're sorry, Mr Sharp. We didn't know Ms Blunt had turned bad.

Mr Sharp: You've all done excellent work!

Kira: Yes, we made a great team in the end.

Akio: Kira and I might just need to smarten up our wardrobes next time we all team up.

Alex: (*pointing at his mud-covered clothes*) A-hem!

Mr Sharp: (*laughing*) Come on. Let's get this bug out of here, and deliver the box to the right people.